ASH WEDNESDAY TO EASTER FOR CHOIRS

COMPILED AND EDITED BY

LIONEL DAKERS & JOHN SCOTT

OXFORD

UNIVERSITY PRESS

OXFORD
UNIVERSITY PRESS

Great Clarendon Street, Oxford OX2 6DP

Oxford University Press is a department of the University of Oxford
and furthers the University's aim of excellence in research, scholarship,
and education by publishing worldwide in

Oxford New York

Athens Auckland Bangkok Bogotá Buenos Aires Calcutta
Cape Town Chennai Dar es Salaam Delhi Florence Hong Kong Istanbul
Karachi Kuala Lumpur Madrid Melbourne Mexico City Mumbai
Nairobi Paris São Paulo Singapore Taipei Tokyo Toronto Warsaw

and associated companies in Berlin Ibadan

Oxford is a registered trademark of Oxford University Press

British Library Cataloguing in Publication Data
Data available

Library of Congress Cataloging-in-Publication Data
Data available

1 3 5 7 9 10 8 6 4 2

ISBN 0–19–353111–9

Music and text origination by
Barnes Music Engraving Ltd., East Sussex.
Printed in Great Britain on acid-free paper by
Halstan & Co. Ltd., Amersham, Bucks.

PREFACE

This collection aims to provide a comprehensive resource-book covering a highly significant part of the Church's year. Its contents span all periods of what is a marvellously rich and uniquely prolific area of church music, and it contains much that is not widely available elsewhere under one cover.

A major policy in compiling the contents has been to ensure that they are relevant to a broad range of musical traditions, with pieces of varying degrees of difficulty to suit the needs and abilities of all choirs. The requirements of the increasing number of small choral groups, as distinct from church and cathedral choirs, have similarly been catered for in the choice of material.

Special features include a number of less familiar works, together with new or recent arrangements of well-known tunes, such as Philip Ledger's 'This joyful Eastertide', Simon Lindley's 'Now the green blade riseth', and Bob Chilcott's setting of 'Were you there?'. Some of the pieces, for example Richard Shephard's 'Sing, my tongue' and Grayston Ives' 'Ride on', have been newly commissioned specifically for this collection, thus filling certain gaps.

Liturgical settings include two versions of the Litany, the Book of Common Prayer text set by the seventeenth-century composer Henry Loosemore, and Philip Marshall's music to the Alternative Service Book text. Other important penitential works are Bairstow's 'The Lamentation' and John Sanders' setting of 'The Reproaches'.

Wherever possible, new practical performing editions of sixteenth-century repertoire have been prepared, reflecting current scholarship and including an English singing translation and, where the original had none, a dynamic scheme. These dynamics are 'terraced' in style, that is the general dynamic levels of phrases are indicated, but hairpins generally avoided. Such dynamics are editorial suggestions only and may be freely ignored or adapted. Note values have in some instances been halved.

We are grateful to The Very Reverend Michael Perham, a member of the Church of England Liturgical Commission, for his invaluable help in encouraging us to include music relevant to the changing liturgical needs of today.

Lionel Dakers
John Scott
August 1998

LITURGICAL PREFACE

One of the most satisfying elements in the liturgical reform of the last thirty years has been the renewal, across the churches, of the celebration of the Christian Year. The infinite variety of the feasts, fasts, and seasons has been recovered, bringing new colour to the liturgy and deepening the experience of those who have shared in it. The cycle of the year has once again become for many a fruitful way into the mystery of God and into the way of Christian discipleship.

If that has been true, to some extent, of the whole year, from Advent through until All Saintstide, it has been true supremely of Holy Week and Easter, and of the season of Lent that prepares for them and the Great Fifty Days to Pentecost that arise from them. Through the liturgy of those days the Christian enters more deeply into the experience of 'dying and rising with Christ'.

This renewal has affected all the churches, but possibly none more so in the British Isles than the Church of England, which, through its 1986 publication, *Lent, Holy Week, Easter*, and through its recent renewal of calendar, lectionary, and collects in *Common Worship* (1997), has embraced this approach with clarity and expectancy. Anglican worship through this period has changed beyond recognition in churches of all traditions.

This has made absolutely necessary the ready availability of music to serve the liturgy through Lent, Holy Week, and Easter. In some cases this means no more than making accessible the riches of the past to churches that have been unaware of them, having had no need of them until the new services created the need for music to enrich the texts. But, in other cases, this has meant the writing of new music to complement new texts.

New insights and approaches are inevitably shared far and wide in the liturgical and musical worlds. Just as the Church of England Liturgical Commission drew widely on the work of Anglicans abroad and the riches of other traditions, so now much of what has been published by the Church of England is being taken up by other churches around the world. The musical resources being made available here without any denominational restriction will make that international process easier.

Both new music and new texts are provided in this collection, catholic in the very best sense, chosen with sensitivity to a variety of needs and with real concern for the mood of the liturgy on each of the crucial days from Ash Wednesday through into the Easter season. The Church will be indebted to Lionel Dakers and John Scott for bringing this collection together at just the moment when it is most needed.

Michael Perham
Derby, August 1998

CONTENTS

Ash Wednesday and Lent

1. Mode V, accomp. Scott	Lent Prose	1
2. Byrd	Civitas sancti tui (Bow thine ear, O Lord)	4
3. Farrant/Hilton	Lord, for thy tender mercy's sake	13
4. Loosemore	The Litany (BCP)	17
5. Marshall	The Litany (ASB)	24
6. Morales	Peccantem me quotidie	27
7. Morley	Agnus Dei	33
8. Rawsthorne	Like as the hart	37
9. Walton	Drop, drop, slow tears	41
10. Wesley	Wash me throughly	45

Passiontide

11. Anerio	Christus factus est	52
12. Bairstow	The Lamentation	55
13. Bairstow/Gibbons	Jesu, grant me this I pray	60
14. Chilcott	God so loved the world	64
15. Händl	Ecce quomodo moritur justus	67
16. Lassus	Adoramus te, Christe	69
17. Stainer	God so loved the world	72

Palm Sunday

18. Bullard	The Feast of Palms	74
19. Gesius	Hosianna dem Sohne Davids	82
20. Hutchings	Hosanna to the Son of David	84
21. Ives	Ride on	87
22. Malcolm	Ingrediente Domino	92
23. Victoria	Pueri Hebraeorum	94

Maundy Thursday

24. plainsong, arr. Barnard	In the heart where love is abiding	100
25. Bruckner	(*a*) Pange lingua	104
	(*b*) Of the glorious Body telling	106
26. de Séverac	Tantum ergo	108
27. Peeters	Ave verum corpus	110
28. Shephard	A new commandment	114
29. Shephard	Sing, my tongue	115

Good Friday

30. Bull	In the departure of the Lord	123
31. spiritual, arr. Chilcott	Were you there?	126
32. Croce	O vos omnes	129
33. trad., arr. Scott	O mortal man	132
34. John IV of Portugal	Crux fidelis	136
35. Morley	Eheu, sustulerunt	139
36. Sanders	The Reproaches	143
37. Victoria	Popule meus	150

Easter

38.	Easter Alleluias	154
	(*a*) Antiphon with psalm tone	
	(*b*) Plainchant Alleluia	
39. Mode VIII, accomp. Scott	I saw water (Vidi aquam)	155
40. Anerio	Alleluia. Christus surrexit	156
41. Bairstow	Psalm 114	165
42. German 1360, arr. Carter	Joy is come!	167
43. Elgar	Light of the World	170
44. Harris	Most glorious Lord of life	182
45. Dutch carol, arr. Ledger	This joyful Eastertide	186
46. French trad., arr. Lindley	Now the green blade riseth	190
47. Rutter	Christ the Lord is risen again!	194
48. Scheidt	Surrexit Christus hodie	202
49. Scott	Easter Anthems	208
50. Shephard	The Easter Song of Praise	212
51. Stanford	Ye choirs of new Jerusalem	216
52. Walford Davies, ed. Dakers	O sons and daughters	225
53. Whitlock	He is risen	229

1. Lent Prose

Mode V
accompaniment by
John Scott

Refrain
(1st time: Cantor)   *(Full)*

VOICES

Hear us, O Lord, have mer-cy up-on us: for we have sin - ned a - gainst thee.
At-ten-de Do-mi-ne, et mi-se-re-re, qui-a pec-ca - vi-mus ti - bi.

ORGAN
(optional)

Verse

1. To thee, Re-deem-er,__ on thy throne of glo - ry: lift we our weep-ing eyes in ho - ly plead-ings:
1. *Ad te Rex sum - me,__ om-ni - um re-demp-tor, o - cu-los no-stros sub-le-va-mus flen - tes:*

lis - ten, O Je - su, to our sup-pli - ca - tions.
ex - au - di, Chri-ste, sup-pli-can-tum pre - ces.

Refrain (Full)

2. O thou chief Cor-ner-stone, Right Hand of the Fa - ther: Way of Sal-va-tion, Gate of Life Ce-les - tial:
2. *Dex-te - ra Pa - tris,_ la - pis an-gu-la - ris, vi-a sa-lu - tis ja-nu-a cae-les - tis,*

Note: verses may be sung by a soloist or semichorus.

16

4. Sins oft com-mit-ted_ now we lay be-fore thee: with true con-tri-tion, now no more we veil them:
4. Ti - bi fa - te - mur_ cri - mi-na ad - mis - sa: con - tri - to cor - de pan - di - mus oc - cul - ta:

18   *Refrain (Full)*

grant us, Re - deem - er, lov - ing ab - so - lu - tion.
tu - a Re - demp - tor, pi - e - tas ig - nos - cat.

19

5. In-no-cent, cap-tive, ta-ken un - re - sist - ing: false-ly ac-cused, and for us   sin-ners sen - tenced,
5. In - no - cens cap-tus,_ nec re-pug-nans duc - tus,   tes - ti-bus fal - sis pro im - pi - is dam-na - tus:

21   *Refrain (Full)*

save us,   we pray thee, Je - su   our Re - deem - er.
quos   re - de - mis - ti,   tu con - ser - va, Chri - ste.

2. Civitas sancti tui

(*Bow thine ear, O Lord*)

Isaiah 64: 10

William Byrd
(1543–1623)
edited by
Watkins Shaw

All dynamics are editorial.

* The 1589 edition of this work places a sharp against this E, an accidental which Watkins Shaw had great difficulty in accepting.

3. Lord, for thy tender mercy's sake

J. Bull

Richard Farrant (*c.*1530–1580)
or John Hilton (*c.*1560–1608)
edited by
Anthony Greening

All dynamics are editorial. May be sung unaccompanied.

4. The Litany

(*BCP*)

from the Whole Service of four and six parts

Book of Common Prayer

Henry Loosemore
(?–1670)
edited by John Cannell

O God the Holy Ghost,
proceeding from the Father and the Son:

have mercy upon us mis - er - a - ble sin - ners.

O God the   Ho - ly Ghost, pro - ceed-ing from the Fa - ther   and the   Son:

Fa-ther and____ the___ Son:

mis - er - a - ble sin - ners.

have mer - cy up - on   us   mis-er-a - ble sin - ners.
mis - er - a - ble sin - ners.

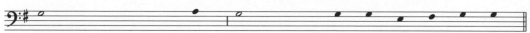

O holy, blessed, and glorious
Trinity, three Persons and one God:

have mercy upon us mis - er - a - ble   sin - ners.

O ho - ly,   bles-sed, and glo-ri - ous_ Tri - ni - ty,   three Per - sons

mis - er - a - ble sin - ners.

and   one God: have mer - cy up - on   us   mis-er-a - ble sin - ners.
mis - er - a - ble sin - ners.

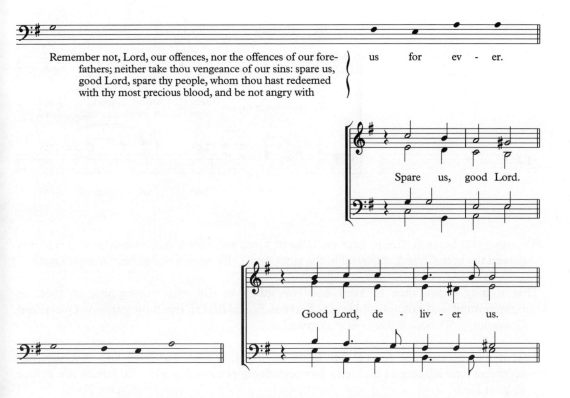

Remember not, Lord, our offences, nor the offences of our fore-
fathers; neither take thou vengeance of our sins: spare us,
good Lord, spare thy people, whom thou hast redeemed
with thy most precious blood, and be not angry with *us for ev - er.*

Spare us, good Lord.

Good Lord, de - liv - er us.

From all evil and mischief; from sin, from the crafts and assaults of the devil; from thy wrath, and from everlasting damnation,   *Good Lord, deliver us.*

From all blindness of heart; from pride, vain-glory, and hypocrisy; from envy, hatred, and malice, and all uncharitableness,   *Good Lord, deliver us.*

From fornication, and all other deadly sin; and from all the deceits of the world, the flesh, and the devil,   *Good Lord, deliver us.*

From lightning and tempest; from plague, pestilence, and famine; from battle and murder, and from sudden death,   *Good Lord, deliver us.*

From all sedition, privy conspiracy, and rebellion; from all false doctrine, heresy, and schism; from hardness of heart, and contempt of thy Word and Commandment,   *Good Lord, deliver us.*

By the mystery of thy holy Incarnation; by thy holy Nativity and Circumcision; by thy Baptism, Fasting, and Temptation,   *Good Lord, deliver us.*

By thine Agony and bloody Sweat; by thy Cross and Passion; by thy precious Death and Burial; by thy glorious Resurrection and Ascension; and by the coming of the Holy Ghost,   *Good Lord, deliver us.*

In all time of our tribulation; in all time of our wealth; in the hour of death, and in the day of judgement,   *Good Lord, deliver us.*

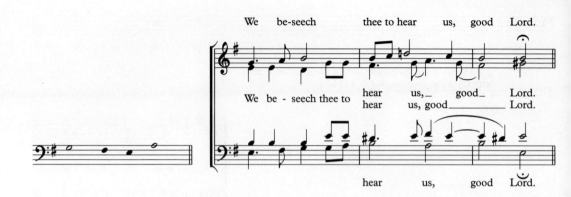

We sinners do beseech thee to hear us, O Lord God; and that it may please thee to rule and govern thy holy Church universal in the right way;   *We beseech thee to hear us, good Lord.*

That it may please thee to keep and strengthen in the true worshipping of thee, in righteousness and holiness of life, thy Servant *ELIZABETH*, our most gracious Queen and Governor;   *We beseech thee to hear us, good Lord.*

That it may please thee to rule her heart in thy faith, fear, and love, and that she may evermore have affiance in thee, and ever seek thy honour and glory;   *We beseech thee to hear us, good Lord.*

That it may please thee to be her defender and keeper, giving her the victory over all her enemies;   *We beseech thee to hear us, good Lord.*

That it may please thee to bless and preserve *Elizabeth* the Queen Mother, *Philip* Duke of *Edinburgh, Charles* Prince of *Wales,* and all the Royal Family;   *We beseech thee to hear us, good Lord.*

That it may please thee to illuminate all Bishops, Priests, and Deacons, with true knowledge and understanding of thy Word; and that both by their preaching and living they may set it forth, and shew it accordingly;   *We beseech thee to hear us, good Lord.*

That it may please thee to endue the Lords of the Council, and all the Nobility, with grace, wisdom, and understanding;   *We beseech thee to hear us, good Lord.*

That it may please thee to bless and keep the Magistrates, giving them grace to execute justice, and to maintain truth;   *We beseech thee to hear us, good Lord.*

That it may please thee to bless and keep all thy people;   *We beseech thee to hear us, good Lord.*

That it may please thee to give to all nations unity, peace, and concord;   *We beseech thee to hear us, good Lord.*

That it may please thee to give us an heart to love and dread thee, and diligently to live after thy commandments;   *We beseech thee to hear us, good Lord.*

That it may please thee to give to all thy people increase of grace to hear meekly thy Word, and to receive it with pure affection, and to bring forth the fruits of the Spirit;   *We beseech thee to hear us, good Lord.*

That it may please thee to bring into the way of truth all such as have erred, and are deceived;   *We beseech thee to hear us, good Lord.*

That it may please thee to strengthen such as do stand; and to comfort and help the weak-hearted; and to raise up them that fall; and finally to beat down Satan under our feet;   *We beseech thee to hear us, good Lord.*

That it may please thee to succour, help, and comfort, all that are in danger, necessity, and tribulation;   *We beseech thee to hear us, good Lord.*

That it may please thee to preserve all that travel by land or by water, all women labouring of child, all sick persons, and young children; and to shew thy pity upon all prisoners and captives;   *We beseech thee to hear us, good Lord.*

That it may please thee to defend, and provide for, the fatherless children, and widows, and all that are desolate and oppressed;   *We beseech thee to hear us, good Lord.*

That it may please thee to have mercy upon all men;   *We beseech thee to hear us, good Lord.*

That it may please thee to forgive our enemies, persecutors, and slanderers, and to turn their hearts;   *We beseech thee to hear us, good Lord.*

That it may please thee to give and preserve to our use the kindly fruits of the earth, so as in due time we may enjoy them;   *We beseech thee to hear us, good Lord.*

That it may please thee to give us true repentence; to forgive us all our sins, negligences, and ignorances; and to endue us with the grace of thy Holy Spirit to amend our lives according to thy holy Word;   *We beseech thee to hear us, good Lord.*

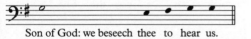

Son of God: we beseech thee to hear us.

O Lamb of God: that takest away the sins of the world;

O Lamb of God: that

that takest a - way the sins of the world,

that takest a - way the sins of the world,

takest a-way the sins of the_____ world, grant us__ thy_____ peace.

that takest a - way the sins of the world,

O Lamb of God: that takest away the sins of the world.

that takest a - way the sins

O   Lamb of God: that takest a - way the
O   Lamb of God: that takest a-way the sins of the_____

O   Lamb of God: that takest a - way the sins

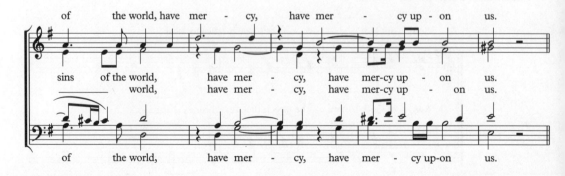

of   the world, have mer - cy,   have mer - cy up - on us.

sins of the world, have mer - cy, have mer-cy up - on us.
_____ world, have mer - cy, have mer-cy up - on us.

of   the world, have mer - cy, have mer - cy up-on us.

Commissioned by the Dean and Chapter of Lincoln Cathedral

5. The Litany
(*ASB*)

Lent, Holy Week, Easter: Services and Prayers

Philip Marshall
(b. 1921)

Choir alone

CANTOR

Let us pray

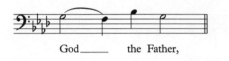

God the Father,

SOPRANO
ALTO

TENOR
BASS

Have mer - cy on us.

God the Son,

Have mer - cy on us.

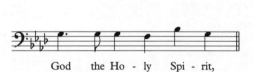

God the Ho - ly Spi - rit,

Have mer - cy on us.

Holy, blessed, and glo - rious Trinity,

Have mer - cy on us.

This setting of the Litany follows the form published within *Lent, Holy Week, Easter: Services and Prayers*, and is a shortened version of the composer's setting of the complete ASB Litany, published by The Church Music Society.

Choir and Congregation *

From all evil and mischief;
from pride, vanity, and hypocrisy;
from envy, hatred, and malice;
and from all e-|vil in-|tent.

From sloth, worldliness, and love of money;
from hardness of heart
and contempt for your word|and your|laws,

From sins of body and mind;
from the deceits of the world,
the flesh,|and the|devil,

Good Lord, de - li - ver us.

In all times of sorrow; in all times of joy;
in the hour of death, and at the|day of|judgement,

By the mystery of your holy incarnation;
by your birth, childhood, and obedience;
by your baptism, fasting,|and temp-|tation,

Good Lord, de - li - ver us.

By your ministry in word and work;
by your mighty acts of power;
and by your preaching|of the|kingdom,

By your agony and trial;
by your cross and passion;
and by your precious|death and|burial,

By your mighty resurrection;
by your glorious ascension;
and by your sending of the|Holy|Spirit,

Good Lord, de - li - ver us.

* The Congregation should join in the repetition of each response, which may be performed by the Choir with closed lips, the final
chord being sustained throughout the following petition.

Choir alone

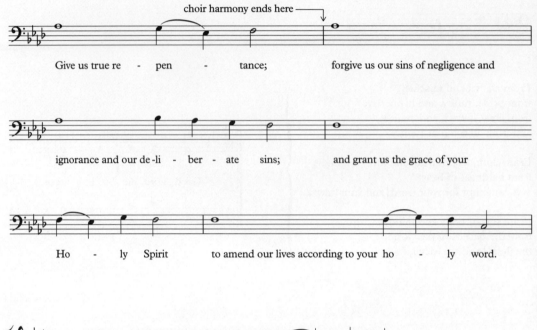

Give us true re - pen - tance; forgive us our sins of negligence and

ignorance and our de -li - ber - ate sins; and grant us the grace of your

Ho - ly Spirit to amend our lives according to your ho - ly word.

Ho - ly God, ho - ly and strong,____

ho - ly and im - mor-tal, have mer - cy up - on____ us.

6. Peccantem me quotidie

Responsory from
Matins for the Dead

Cristobal Morales
(c.1500–1553)
edited by
Timothy Morris

All dynamics are editorial.

7. Agnus Dei

Thomas Morley
(1557–1603)
edited by
John Milsom

All dynamics are editorial.

8. Like as the hart

Psalm 42: 1–3

Noel Rawsthorne
(b. 1929)

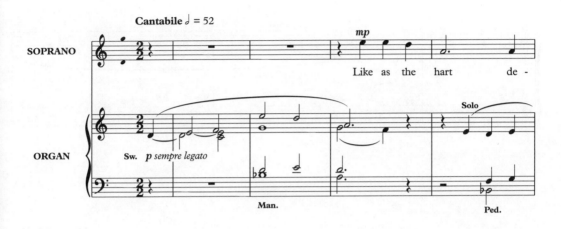

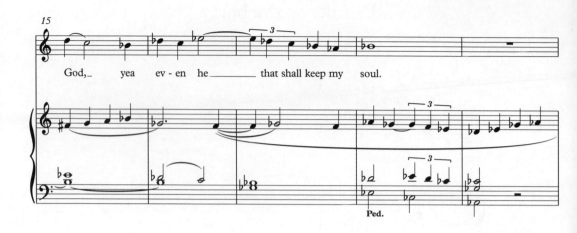

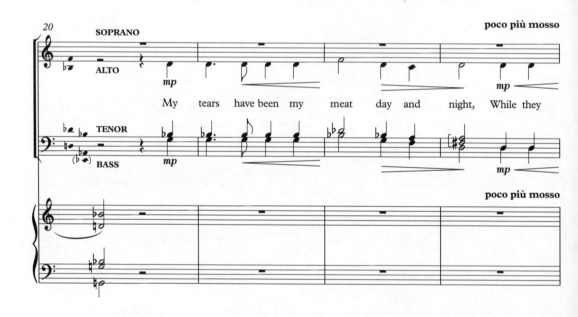

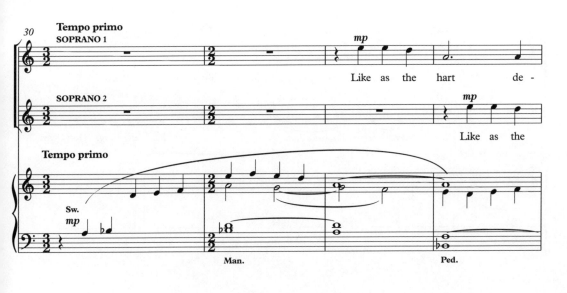

9. A Litany
(*Drop, drop, slow tears*)

Phineas Fletcher

William Walton
(1902–1983)
edited by
Tim Brown

10. Wash me throughly

Psalm 51: 2–3

Samuel Sebastian Wesley
(1810–1876)

11. Christus factus est

Gradual for Maundy Thursday
English text by Paul England

Felice Anerio
(*c*.1560–1614)
edited by
John Rutter

All dynamics are editorial.

* This ♯ is in the source, but a C♮ may be thought preferable here.

† C in source.

12. The Lamentation

Words selected from
the Lamentations of Jeremiah
by Eric Milner-White

Edward C. Bairstow
(1874–1946)
edited by
Lionel Dakers and John Scott

The prophet mourneth for the sins of the people of God.

1. *p* How doth the city sit solitary that was | full of | people:
   how is she be-|come | as a | widow.

2. *mf* She that was great among the nations and princess a-|mong the | provin·ces:
   how is | she be-|come | tribu·tary.

3. *p* She weepeth sore in the night ∗ and her tears are | on her | cheeks:
   among all her lovers | she hath | none to | comfort · her.

4. The ways of Zi-|on do | mourn:
   because none come to the | solemn as-|sembly.

5. All her | gates are | deso·late:
   and she her-|self is in | bitter·ness.

6. The Lord hath afflicted her for the multitude of | her trans-|gressions:
   her children are gone into captivity be-|fore · the | ene·my.

Performance notes: Bar-lines in the verses correspond to bar-lines in the music. Asterisks indicate breaks (e.g. v. 3). A dot dividing the syllables of a word or placed between two words indicates how two or more notes are to be divided. A horizontal rule over a word or syllable (e.g. v. 6) indicates that two notes are sung to it.
  The dots over the words 'and the' in v. 17 indicate that these words are sung to one note. Verses 11 and 25 carry through the middle of the chant; break only at the asterisk.

VOICES IN UNISON

7. All they that go by clap their hands at her:

they hiss and wag their head at the daughter of Je - ru - sa - lem saying:

8. 'Is this the city that men called the per - fec-tion of beauty: the joy of the whole earth?'

Man.

Ped.

REFRAIN

Largo espressivo

Je - ru - sa-lem,___ Je - ru - sa-lem,___ re - turn un - to the Lord thy God.

Largo espressivo

Christ recalleth us to God by his passion.

9. *p*   For these | things I | weep:
         mine eye, mine | eye · runneth | down with | water.

10.   From on high hath the Lord sent fire into my bones *
       and it prevail-|eth a-|gainst them:
       he hath made me | deso·late and | faint · all the | day.

11.   My flesh and my | skin hath | he made || old: *|
       he hath | broken · my | bones.

12.   He hath build-|ed a-|gainst me:
       and compass'd | me with | gall and | travail.

13.   He hath made me to dwell | in dark | places:
       as those | that have | been long | dead.

14.   I am become a derision to | all my | people:
       and their | song all the | day.

15.   Let him give his cheek to | him that | smiteth him:
       Let him be filled | full with re-|proach.

16. *pp* Is it nothing to you all ye | that pass | by:
         behold and see if there be any sorrow | like unto | my sorrow.

17.   Remember mine affliction | and my | misery:
       the | worm-wood and the | gall.

REFRAIN

Je - ru - sa - lem,_____ Je - ru - sa - lem,_____

_____ re - turn un - to the Lord_____ thy God.

The church repenteth and turneth again.

18. *p*   Remember O Lord what is | come up- | on us:
         behold and | see our re- | proach.

19.   The joy of our | heart is | ceas'd;
      our | dance is | turn'd into | mourning.

20.   The crown is fallen | from our | head:
      woe unto us | for we have | sinn'd.

21.   For this our | heart is | faint:
      for | these things · our | eyes · are | dim.

22.   Let us search and | try our | ways:
and turn again | unto the | Lord.

23.   Turn thou us unto thee O Lord and we | shall be | turn'd:
re- | new our | days as of | old.

24.   It is of the Lord's mercies that we are | not con- | sum'd:
because his com- | p͞a͞s·sions | fail not.

25. *mf* They are new | ever·y | morn- | | ing: * |
great | i͞s · thy | faithfulness.

26.   The Lord is my portion | saith my | soul:
cresc. therefore will I | h͞o͞pe · in | him.

27.   O Lord thou hast pleaded the causes | of my | soul:
f   thou | hast re- | d͞e͞e͞m'd · my | life.

REFRAIN

13. Jesu, grant me this I pray

17th-century Latin
tr. H. W. Baker

Orlando Gibbons
(1583–1625)
With verses in Fauxbourdon
by Edward C. Bairstow
(1874–1946)

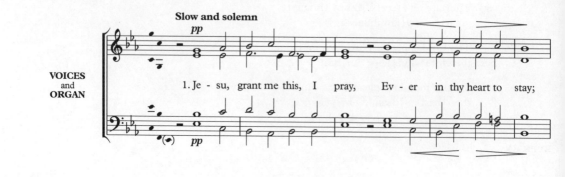

This hymn may be sung in the following ways:

1. As an anthem by the choir, preferably without organ.

2. The congregation may join in verses 1, 3, and 4; but in this case the music of verse 1 must be used for verse 4.

3. The fauxbourdon for the choir may be played on the organ and the choir may sing in unison in verses 2 and 3, or in verse 3 only.

I am safe when I a - bide   In thy_ heart and wound - ed side.

I am_ safe when I a - bide_   In thy heart and wound-ed side.

Più animato

SOPRANO

3. If__ the flesh,_ more__ dan - gerous still,

ALTO

3. If__ the flesh,_____ more dan-gerous still,_____ Tempt my

TENOR *f*

3. If   the flesh,   more   dan - gerous still,

BASS *mf*

3. If   the flesh,   more   dan - gerous still, Tempt my

Più animato

4. Death will come to me one day; Je - su, cast me not_ a - way:_ Dy - ing
let me still_ a - bide____ In thy_ heart and wound-ed side._ A - men.

* Alternative bass:

Commissioned in memory of Dan and Pat Jacobson by Jeanne Jacobson Stephens and Gary Stephens for the Lovers Lane United Methodist Sanctuary Choir, Dallas, Texas

14. God so loved the world

John 3: 16

Bob Chilcott
(b. 1955)

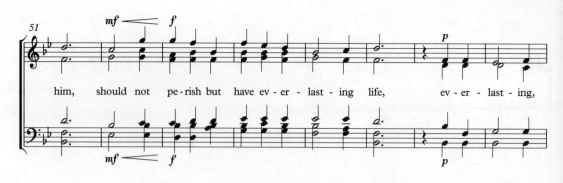

him,   should not   pe-rish but   have ev - er - last - ing   life,   ev - er - last - ing,

SOPRANO SOLO

ev - er - last - ing   life,   ev - er -

ev - er - last - ing,   God   so   loved   the   world,_____

ev - er - last - ing   life._____   God   so

- last - ing   life,   God   so   loved   the   world.

___   God   so   loved   the   world,   so   loved   the   world.

loved   the   world,_____   God   so   loved   the   world.

15. Ecce quomodo moritur justus

Isaiah 57: 1–2
English translation by Timothy Morris

Jacob Händl (Gallus)
(1550–1591)
edited by
Andrew Parker

PART I

SOPRANO
ALTO

TENOR
BASS

Ec - ce, quo - mo-do mo - ri - tur ju - - - stus,
Be - hold, see___ how the just___ man di - - - eth,

et ne - mo per - ci - pit cor - de, et ne - mo per - ci - pit cor - de; vi -
and no - one ta - keth it to heart, and no - one ta - keth it to heart; how

- ri ju - sti tol-lun - tur, et___ ne - mo con - si - de - rat; a fa - ci - e i -
___ the just men are ta - ken, and___ no - one con - si - de - reth; be - fore the face of

- ni - qui - ta - tis, sub - la - tus est ju - stus et e - rit in pa - ce
this world's e - vil the___ good man is ta - ken, in peace and tran-qui - li-ty

All dynamics are editorial.

16. Adoramus te, Christe

Antiphon at Feasts of the Holy Cross
English translation by John Rutter

Orlande de Lassus
(1532–1594)
edited by
John Rutter

All dynamics are editorial.

17. God so loved the world

from *The Crucifixion*

John 3: 16

John Stainer
(1840–1901)

This anthem may be sung as a solo Quartet.

18. The Feast of Palms

G. Moultrie

Alan Bullard
(b. 1947)

* The organ may lightly double the choir in the unaccompanied sections, if desired.

-san-nah, ho - san - nah, ho - san-nah   in   the   high - est,   in   the   high - est!

They   set   him   on____   his throne so   rude;   Be - fore   him   went

____ the mul - ti - tude,   And   in____   their____   way   their   gar - ments strewed:

Ho - san-nah, ho - san - nah, ho - san-nah in the high - est,

in the high - est!   They

S./A. *f*

T./B. *f*   They thronged be - fore,

più f

thronged   be - fore,___   be - hind, a - round,   They   threw   palm - branch-

___   be - hind, a - round,   They   threw   palm - branch - es   on the

19. Hosianna dem Sohne Davids

German text anon.
English text by Elwood Coggin

Bartholomäus Gesius
(*c*.1560–1613)
edited by
Elwood Coggin

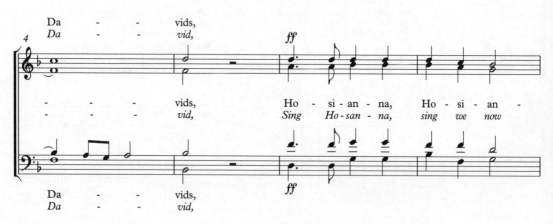

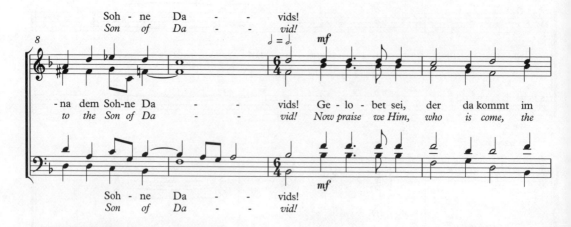

All dynamics are editorial.

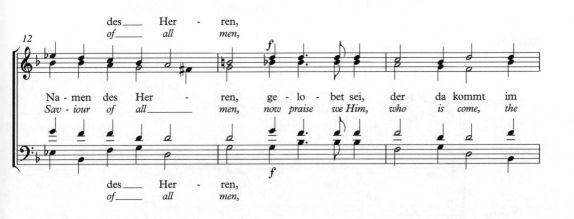

20. Hosanna to the Son of David

Matthew 21: 9

Arthur Hutchings
(1906–1989)

Note values of the original have been halved.

21. Ride on

Henry Milman

Grayston Ives
(b. 1948)

of the sky look down with sad and__ won - d'ring eyes_____ to

poco rit. **a tempo**

see the ap-proach-ing sac - ri - fice._____ Ride on, ride on in

Ride on, ride on in

ma - jes - ty,_____ ride on in ma - jes - ty!_____ Thy

22. Ingrediente Domino

Antiphon from Palm Sunday Procession

George Malcolm
(1917–1998)

23. Pueri Hebraeorum

Matthew 21: 8, 9

Tomas Luis de Victoria
(*c*.1548–1611)
edited by
Timothy Morris

All dynamics are editorial.

24. In the heart where love is abiding

Words by Paul Wigmore
based on *Ubi caritas et amor*
from the Latin liturgy for Maundy Thursday

Traditional plainsong melody
arranged by
John Barnard
(b. 1948)

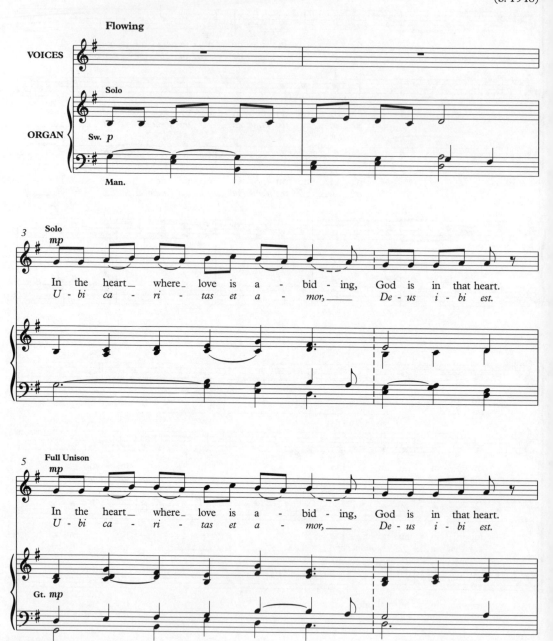

This piece may be sung in unison, but antiphonal effects should be preserved – solo/choir, sopranos/men, or two semi-choruses of equal voices, as appropriate. When sung in unison, the alto/bass parts of the final refrain should be used. If necessary, the staggered Amens may both be sung at soprano or bass pitch.

25(a). Pange lingua

St Thomas Aquinas

Anton Bruckner
(1824–1896)

Dynamics at performers' discretion.

2. Nobis datus, nobis natus
   Ex intacta Virgine,
   Et in mundo conversatus,
   Sparso verbi semine,
   Sui moras incolatus
   Miro clausit ordine.

3. In supremae nocte coenae
   Recumbens cum fratribus,
   Observata lege plene
   Cibis in legalibus,
   Cibum turbae duodenae
   Se dat suis manibus.

4. Verbum caro, panem verum
   Verbo carnem efficit,
   Fitque sanguis Christi merum,
   Et si sensus deficit,
   Ad firmandum cor sincerum
   Sola fides sufficit.

   Part 2 *Tantum ergo*

5. Tantum ergo Sacramentum
   Veneremur cernui,
   Et antiquum documentum
   Novo cedat ritui:
   Praestet fides supplementum
   Sensuum defectui.

6. Genitori, Genitoque
   Laus et jubilatio,
   Salus, honor, virtus quoque
   Sit et benedictio:
   Procedenti ab utroque
   Compar sit laudatio.

25(*b*). Of the glorious Body telling

St Thomas Aquinas
tr. J. M. Neale and others

Anton Bruckner
(1824–1896)

1. Of the glo - rious Bo - dy tell - ing, O my tongue, its

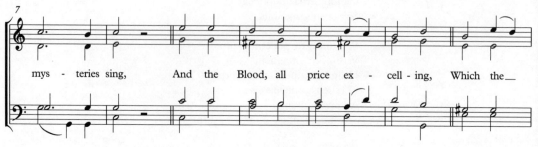

mys - teries sing, And the Blood, all price ex - cell - ing, Which the__

world's e - ter - nal King, In a no - ble womb once dwell - ing, Shed for

this__ world's ran - som - ing, Shed for this world's ran - som - ing.

Dynamics at performers' discretion.

2. Giv'n for us, for us descending,
    Of a virgin to proceed,
    Man with man in converse blending,
    Scattered he the gospel seed,
    Till his sojourn drew to ending,
    Which he closed in wondrous deed.

3. At the last great supper lying
    Circled by his brethren's band,
    Meekly with the law complying,
    First he finished its command,
    Then, immortal food supplying,
    Gave himself with his own hand.

4. Word-made-flesh, by word he maketh
    Bread his very Flesh to be;
    Man in wine Christ's Blood partaketh:
    And if senses fail to see,
    Faith alone the true heart waketh
    To behold the mystery.

    Part 2 *Tantum ergo*

5. Therefore we, before him bending,
    This great Sacrament revere;
    Types and shadows have their ending,
    For the newer rite is here;
    Faith, our outward sense befriending,
    Makes the inward vision clear.

6. Glory let us give, and blessing
    To the Father and the Son;
    Honour, might, and praise addressing,
    While eternal ages run;
    Ever too his love confessing,
    Who from both, with both is one.

26. Tantum ergo

St Thomas Aquinas
English text by Kerry Beaumont

Déodat de Séverac
(1873–1921)

27. Ave verum corpus

14th-century hymn, sometimes attributed
to Pope Innocent VI

Flor Peeters
(1903–1986)

28. A new commandment

John 13: 34–5

Richard Shephard
(b. 1949)

29. Sing, my tongue

Venantius Fortunatus
tr. J. M. Neale and others

Richard Shephard
(b. 1949)

cross,_ the vic-tor's tro - phy, sound the high_ tri-um-phal lay,_

SOPRANO   *mp*   *cresc.*   *f*

how, the pains of death   en - dur-ing,   earth's_ Re-deem - er   won_____ the_

day.

30. In the departure of the Lord

Sir William Leighton

John Bull
(1563–1628)
edited by
Timothy Morris

All dynamics are editorial.

31. Were you there?

Spiritual
arr. Bob Chilcott
(b. 1955)

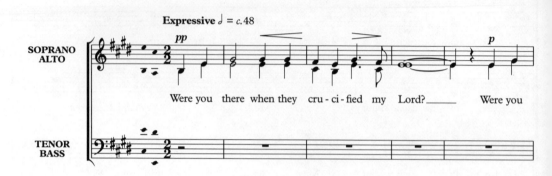

Were you there when they cru-ci-fied my Lord?____ Were you

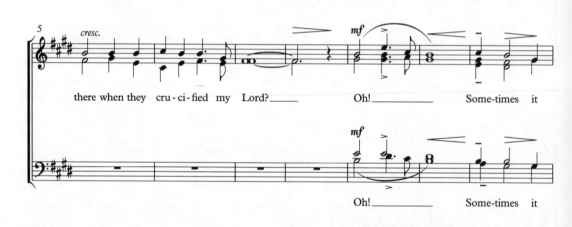

there when they cru-ci-fied my Lord?____ Oh!_____ Some-times it

Oh!_____ Some-times it

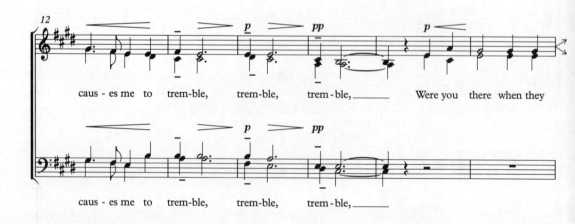

caus-es me to trem-ble, trem-ble, trem-ble,____ Were you there when they

caus-es me to trem-ble, trem-ble, trem-ble,____

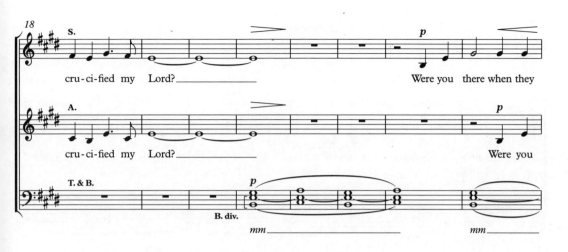

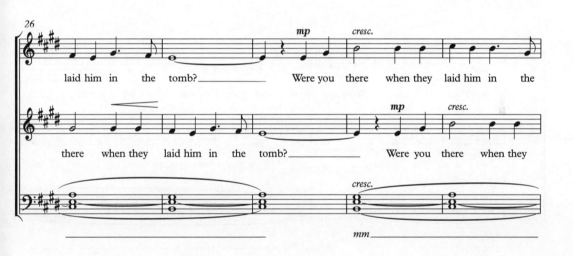

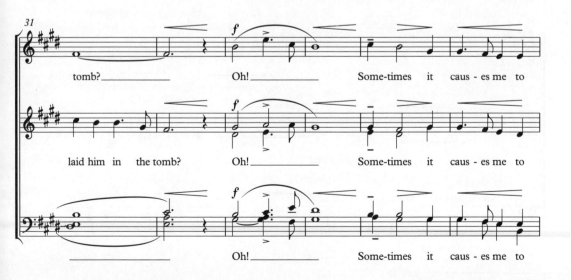

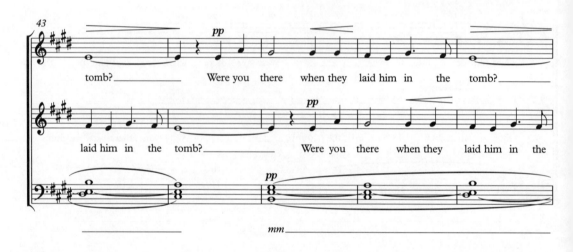

32. O vos omnes

Lamentations 1: 12

Giovanni Croce
(1557–1609)
edited by
Timothy Morris

All dynamics are editorial.

33. O mortal man

(Sussex Mummers' Carol)

Words traditional

Traditional melody
arranged by
John Scott
(b. 1956)

1. O__ mor-tal__ man, re - mem-ber well, when Christ our__ Lord was__

The melody was collected from the neighbourhood of Horsham *c.*1876 by Lucy Broadwood. Verse 1 may be sung unaccompanied.
Verse 2 may be sung by a soprano (or tenor) solo, with the other voices singing to 'Ah' or humming, or with organ accompaniment only.
Verse 2 may also be sung unaccompanied. The descant to the last verse is optional.

born,_____ He was cru - ci - fied_ be - tween two_ thieves, and crown - ed with the_

thorn,_____ and crown - ed_ with_____ the thorn._

Ch. or Solo

2. O_ mor-tal man, re - mem-ber well, when

Ah_____

35 **OPTIONAL DESCANT**

Ah_____

mor - tal man, re - mem - ber well, when Christ was wrapped in_____ clay,_____ He was

Sw. *p*

39

tak - en to__ a se - pul - chre where no man ev - er__ lay,_____ where

43

no__ man ev - er lay.__

Solo

p

Sw.

Flute

pp

Celeste

(32')

34. Crux fidelis

Words attributed to Venantius Fortunatus
tr. John Rutter

attributed to
John IV, King of Portugal
(1604–1656)
edited by
John Rutter

for rehearsal only

All dynamics are editorial.

35. Eheu, sustulerunt

John 20: 13

Thomas Morley
(1557–1603)
edited by
Timothy Morris

All dynamics are editorial.

36. The Reproaches

Holy Week Services

John Sanders
(b. 1933)

A. O MY PEOPLE

This is a reduced version of the original 8-part setting (available from the RSCM). It may be sung unaccompanied or with the organ providing support if needed. The verses should if possible be sung unaccompanied, even when the organ is used in sections A, B, and C.

Verse 1

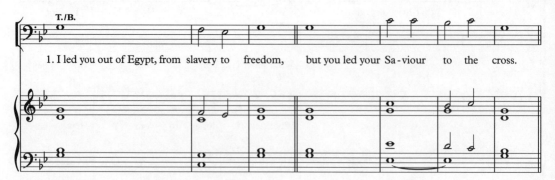

1. I led you out of Egypt, from slavery to freedom, but you led your Sa-viour to the cross.

B. O MY PEOPLE

C. HOLY IS GOD

Verse 2

2. For forty years I led you safely through the desert. I fed you with manna from heaven,

and brought you to a land of plenty: but you led your Sa - viour to the cross.

Repeat **C. HOLY IS GOD**

Verse 3

3. What more could I have done for you?* I planted you as my fair - est vine,

but you yielded on - ly bitterness: When I was thirsty you gave me vinegar to drink,

and you pierced your Saviour's side with a lance.

Repeat **C. HOLY IS GOD**

Verse 4

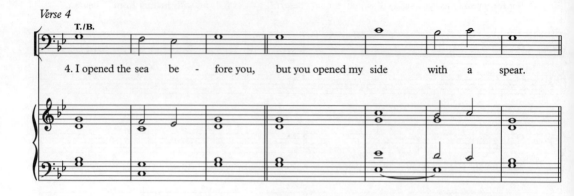

4. I opened the sea be - fore you, but you opened my side with a spear.

Verse 5

5. I led you on your way in a pillar of cloud, but you led me to Pi - late's court.

Repeat **B. O MY PEOPLE**

Verse 6

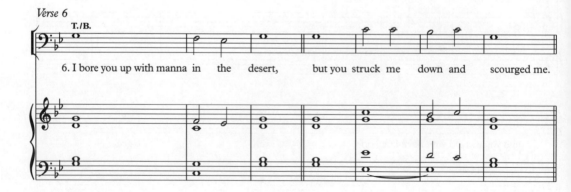

6. I bore you up with manna in the desert, but you struck me down and scourged me.

Verse 7

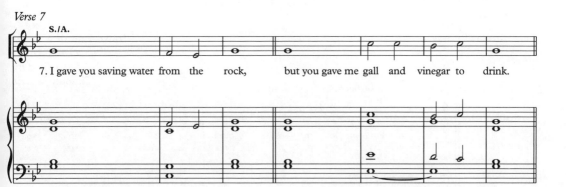

7. I gave you saving water from the rock, but you gave me gall and vinegar to drink.

Repeat **B. O MY PEOPLE**

Verse 8

8. I gave you a roy - al sceptre, but you gave me a crown of thorns.

Verse 9

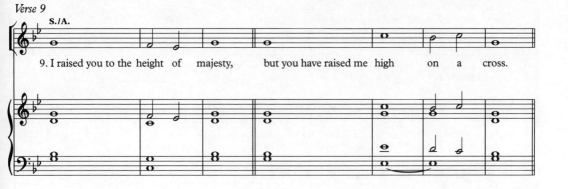

9. I raised you to the height of majesty, but you have raised me high on a cross.

Repeat **A. O MY PEOPLE**

37. Popule meus

Good Friday Liturgy

Tomás Luis de Victoria
(1548–1611)
edited by
Timothy Morris

All dynamics are editorial.

* The directions for Choirs I and II may be ignored and the choral sections sung by the full choir throughout.

Verse 1

mf SOLO

1. Qui - a e - du - xi te__ de__ ter-ra_____ Ae - gy - pti,
1. I_____ led you__ out_ of E - gypt, __ from sla-ve-ry_____ to__ free-dom,

pa - ra - - - sti cru - cem_____ sal - va-to - ri tu - o._____
but__ you_____ led your Sa - viour to____ the_____ cross. _____

11 (CHOIR II) *f*   (CHOIR I) *p*

A - gi - os o The - os.   San - ctus   De - us.
Ho - ly   is   God.

A - gi - os o The - os.   San - ctus   De - us.
Ho - ly   is   God.

A - gi - os o The - os.   San - ctus   De - us.
Ho - ly   is   God.

A - gi - os o The - os.   San - ctus   De - us.
Ho - ly   is   God.

18 (CHOIR II) *f*   (CHOIR I) *p*

A - gi - os is - chy - ros.   San - ctus   for - tis.
Ho - ly   and   strong.

A - gi - os is - chy - ros.   San - ctus   for - tis.
Ho - ly   and   strong.

A - gi - os is - chy - ros.   San - ctus   for - tis.
Ho - ly   and   strong.

A - gi - os is - chy - ros.   San - ctus   for - tis.
Ho - ly   and   strong.

38. Easter Alleluias

(a) Antiphon with psalm tone

(b) Plainchant Alleluia

39. I saw water

(Vidi aquam)

Words from Ezekiel 47

Mode VIII (adapted)
accompaniment by
John Scott

40. Alleluia. Christus surrexit

1 Cor. 15: 20–2

Felice Anerio
(c.1560–1614)
edited by
Timothy Morris

for
rehearsal
only

All dynamics are editorial.

41. Psalm 114

Edward C. Bairstow
(1874–1946)

1. When Israel came out of Egypt: and the house of Jacob from a - mong the strange people,

2. Judah was his sanctuary and Is - rael his do - minion.

3. The sea saw that and fled: Jor - dan was dri - ven back.

4. The mountains skipped like rams: and the little hills like young sheep.

5. What aileth thee O thou sea that thou fleddest: and thou Jordan that thou wast dri - ven back?

6. Ye mountains that ye skipped like rams: and ye little hills, like young sheep?

7. Tremble thou earth at the presence of the Lord: at the presence of the God of Jacob;

Org.
ff
(32′ reed)

8. Who turned the hard rock into a standing water: and the flintstone in - to a spring-ing well.

Glory be to the Father, and to the Son, and to the Ho - ly Ghost;

As it was in the be - ginning is now and ever shall be, world with-out end. A - men.

42. Joy is come!

Words by Andrew Carter

Tune: German 1360
arranged by
Andrew Carter
(b. 1939)

1. Joy is come! Eas-ter-tide! Sing we all far and wide, See the stone rolled a-side, Christ our Lord is ris-en, Burst-ing from his pri-son. Let the sound, sound, sound, Ring a-round, round, round, And the song now re-bound: Christ the Lord is ris-en!

2. Joy is come! Eas-ter Day! Join the dance, hom-age pay, Christ the Lord lights our way, From the tomb now break-ing,_ Sa-tan's pow-er shak-ing. Let the song, song, song, E-cho long, long, long, Shout it loud, sing it strong: Christ the Lord is ris-en!

43. Light of the World

from *The Light of Life*

Words: E. Capel-Cure

Edward Elgar
(1857–1934)
organ reduction by
John Scott

44. Most glorious Lord of life

Edmund Spenser

William H. Harris
(1883–1973)

for Annetta Heeran

45. This joyful Eastertide

G. R. Woodward

Dutch carol
arr. Philip Ledger
(b. 1937)

Music © 1994 Encore Publications. Reproduced by permission. Text © A. R. Mowbray, an imprint of Cassell plc. Available separately from Encore Publications, 22 Tonbridge Road, Hildenborough, Kent TN11 9BS, England.

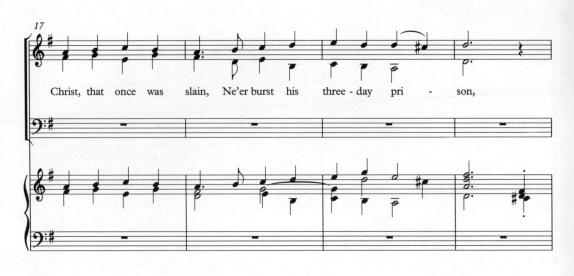

Christ, that once was slain, Ne'er burst his three - day pri - son,

Our faith had been in vain:

Man.

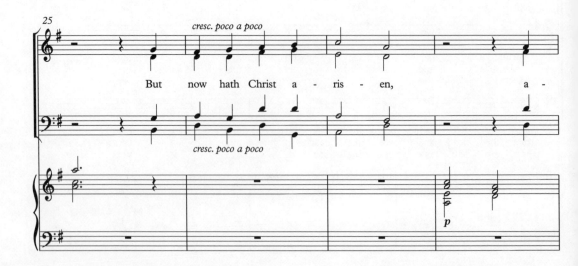

cresc. poco a poco

But now hath Christ a - ris - en, a -

cresc. poco a poco

46. Now the green blade riseth

J. M. C. Crum

French trad.
arr. Simon Lindley
(b. 1948)

With much expression and flow (♩ = *c.* 72)

SOPRANO
ALTO

TENOR
BASS

mp legato

Ped.

SOPRANOS
mp espress.

Now the green blade ris - eth from the — bur - ied grain.

Wheat — that in dark earth ma - ny — days has lain;

poco rit.

Love lives a - gain, that with the dead has been:

a tempo

Love is come a - gain, like wheat that spring-eth green.

Man.

SOLO (*any voice*)
mf espress.

In the grave they laid him, Love whom men had slain,

mf

Ped.

espress.

Think - ing that ne - ver he would wake a - gain,

47. Christ the Lord is risen again!

Michael Weisse
tr. Catherine Winkworth

John Rutter
(b. 1945)

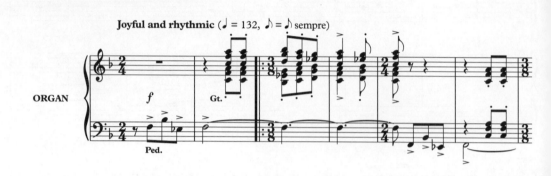

48. Surrexit Christus hodie

Words tr. John Rutter

Samuel Scheidt
(1587–1654)
edited by
John Rutter

All dynamics are editorial.

49. Easter Anthems

Book of Common Prayer

John Scott
(b. 1956)

1. Christ our passover is sacri-ficed for us: therefore let us keep the feast;

2. Not with the óld leaven,* nor with the leaven of malice and wickedness: —

but with the únleavened bread of sin - ce - ri - ty and truth. _____

3. Christ being raised from the dead dieth no more: death hath no more do-min-ion over him.

4.* For in that he died, he died unto sin once: but in that he liveth, he liveth unto God.

Man.   Ped.

5.* Likewise reckon ye also yourselves to be dead in - deed unto sin:

Man.

* The first half of verses 4 and 5 may also be sung A.T.B. or S.A.B.

but alive unto God through Je - sus Christ our Lord.

Ped.

6. Christ is risen from the dead: and become the first-fruits of them that slept.

7. For since by man came death: by man came also the resur -rec - tion of the dead.

Man.

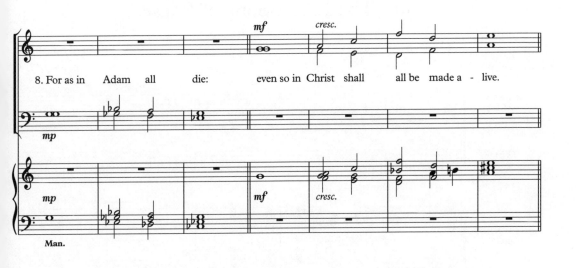

8. For as in Adam all die: even so in Christ shall all be made a - live.

Man.

Glory be to the Father, and to the Son:__ and to the Ho - ly Ghost;

Ped.

optional

as it was in the beginning is now and ever shall be: world without end. A - - men.

50. The Easter Song of Praise

Richard Shephard
(b. 1949)

13

Christ   is   ri - sen from   the grave!   Sa - lute your king in

17   *più legato*   *mp*

glo-rious sym-pho - ny.   Sing choirs of   earth!   Be -

dim.   *mp*   *più legato*   *unacc. ad lib.*

Sw.   *mp*

Man.   Ped.   Man.

22

-hold your light has   come!___   The_   glo - ry   of   the   Lord shines ra - diant -

-ult with joy out-poured. The_ gos - pel trum - pets_ tell of vic - t'ry

won! Your Sa - viour lives: he's with you ev - er-more! Let

all God's peo - ple shout the long A - men. A - men.

51. Ye choirs of new Jerusalem

St Fulbert of Chartres,
tr. R. Campbell and others

C. V. Stanford
(1852–1924)

52. O sons and daughters

J. Tisserand
tr. J. M. Neale

H. Walford Davies
(1869–1941)
edited by
Lionel Dakers
(b. 1924)

* To be sung in speech rhythm until organ enters at bar 43. The music is based on a 17th-century French melody.

* Optional manual notes.

53. He is risen

Mrs C. F. Alexander

Percy Whitlock
(1903–1946)

Let the whole wide earth re - joice, the whole wide earth re - joice.

whole, the whole wide

Death is con-quered, Man is free, Christ has won the

vic - to-ry. Come, ye sad__ and fear - ful - heart - ed,